On the Party by Liu Shaoqi
First Prism Key Press Edition 2011

Prism Key Press
New York, NY 10001
PrismKeyPress.com

ISBN-13: 978-1466378421

On the Party

Liu Shaoqi

CONTENTS

1. Introduction

May 14, 1945
Comrades,

In his report to the Seventh National Congress of the Party, Comrade Mao Zedong made a penetrating and brilliant analysis of the present international and domestic situation. (192) He comprehensively summed up the eight years of the Chinese People's War of Resistance Against Japan and the line persistently followed by our Party in this war. He formulated a great programme of common struggle for the Chinese people and for all democratic parties and groups throughout the country, which shows both the way to mobilize and unite all the forces of the Chinese people for the final defeat of the Japanese aggressors and the way to build an independent, free, democratic, united, prosperous and powerful new China after their defeat.

Comrade Mao Zedong's report is a militant call to the Chinese people for victory. It is a Magna Charta for the building of a new-democratic-republic.

Over the past twenty-four years of heroic struggle and especially in the heroic war of presence of the past eight years, our Party, has together with together with the Chinese people, traveled a torturous path amidst countless difficulties and hardships. Under the leadership of Comrade Mao Zedong, it has finally achieved brilliant success and opened up the prospect of a bright future for the Chinese nation and people. Our Party has, together with the Liberated Areas, the eight route Army (55), the New Fourth Army (117) and the other armed forces of the people under its leadership, become the cornerstone of the effort by the whole country to resist Japan and save the nation.

The reason why our Party has been able to achieve these

tremendous successes is that from the very beginning it had been a proletarian party of an entirely new type — a party dedicated whole-heartedly to serving the Chinese people and built upon the very solid theoretical foundation of sinified Marxism-Leninism. Having adopted Mao Zedong Thought — the theory which integrates Marxism-Leninism with the practice of the Chinese revolution — as the guide in all its work, our Party has formulated a revolutionary programme and revolutionary policies which fully represent the interests of the Chinese nation and people. It has not only waged a resolute struggle against the enemies of the Chinese nation and people and against all the reactionary political groups that act contrary to their interests, but has also crushed every kind of opportunism within the Party itself. It is under the guidance of the great Mao Zedong Thought that our Party has gathered together the most loyal, courageous, politically conscious and well-disciplined representatives of the Chinese working class and labouring people. And in doing so, the Party has become the organized vanguard of the Chinese working class, fighting most resolutely and bravely against the enemies of the Chinese nation and people and successfully striking at these enemies while avoiding their blows.

Our Party owes its great success to the fact that it has consistently carried out its fundamental principle of serving the people, which has enabled it to take root among the masses of the people, maintain close ties with them and become a well-disciplined party. It is a party which practices strict centralism on a democratic basis. It is a party which voluntarily observes iron discipline and seriously conducts criticism and self-criticism. It is a party which does not allow small groups or factions to operate within it, and it is a party which admits new members with care, demanding that each member take a direct part in a Party organization and in Party work. All such organizational principles aim at leading the people to complete emancipation. These have been embodied in our Party Constitution since its adoption by the First National Congress of the Party and have been fully borne out in the great practical struggles of the past twenty-four years. These principles on which our Party is organized not only guarantee the fulfillment of its political tasks, its unity of action in struggle and its conquest of every kind of difficulty, but also guarantee that great victories will be won by the people under Party leadership.

The broad revolutionary masses of the Chinese people enthusiastically welcome and trust such a party as ours, not only because it adheres to a revolutionary programme and revolutionary policies that fully respect the interests of the Chinese people, but also because it has a closely-knit organization and iron discipline, is capable of surviving severe, trying battles and has demonstrated its impregnable organizational strength. In the face of a powerful, cunning and barbarous enemy, the struggle for the liberation of the disaster-ridden Chinese nation with its 475 million people is an exceedingly momentous undertaking. Only a party like ours has the ability and daring to lead the entire people in defeating our enemies and winning liberation. The revision of our Party Constitution today does not involve any change in the character or in the fundamental organizational principles of our Party. On the contrary, by revising we intend to develop and strengthen that character and those principles on the basis of recent experience and on the theory of Party building enriched by Comrade Mao Zedong during the past three great revolutionary periods. Obviously, it is absolutely necessary to do so in order to enormously increase the fighting capacity of our Party, cement our ties with the broad masse of the Chinese people, get prepared for the great events which lie ahead, bring about the final defeat of the Japanese aggressors and their lackeys and build an independent, free, democratic, united prosperous and powerful new-democratic republic.

However, the Constitution - that is to say the rules and regulations of our Party - not only defines the fundamental principles governing the Party but also lays down, in line with these principles, the methods of practical action for the Party organization and the rules governing the organizational forms of Party structure and inner-Party life. Because the organizational forms and methods of work of the Party are determined by the internal and external conditions in which it finds itself and by the political tasks it sets, a certain degree of flexibility must be allowed. When the Party defines new political tasks because of changes in circumstances or in working conditions, the organizational forms and methods of work have to be changed accordingly; otherwise old organizational forms and old methods of work will hinder the progress of the Party's work and the performance of our political tasks. Our Party is a creative Marxist political party, because at no time have we tied ourselves ideologically or politically to any rigid formulas, or regarded the organizational forms of our Party or any other organizational forms as hard fast patterns that cannot be altered. From time to time, we have been able to improve our organizational forms and our methods of work in accordance with the changing conditions and in the development of the Chinese revolution and with our new political tasks and freshly acquired experience in our organizational work. Therefore, given the fundamental organizational principles of our Party, it is entirely necessary to revise our Party Constitution in light of the new environment and conditions and the changed situation in the Party.

The Party firmly upholds the inviolability of its fundamental organizational principles. However, it must adapt its organizational forms and methods of work to the existing circumstances so as to promote progress in the Party's work and ensure the completion of its political tasks and its unity of action.

We propose to the Seventh National Congress of the Party many important changes and additions to the Party Constitution. Why is it necessary to make such changes and additions? The reasons are as follows:

1. It is now seventeen years since our Party

10

Constitution was revised in 1928 by the Sixth National Congress.(151) Conditions both inside and outside the Party have changed significantly during these years. Today the Party is faced with the need to mobilize the whole Party membership to carry out entirely new political tasks.

2. The experience which our Party has accumulated in directing the revolutionary struggle in China during the last seventeen years is extremely rich and vitally important. It is essential to sum up this experience and use it to enrich our Party Constitution and to strengthen the building of our Party.

3. Because the Party Constitution was adopted by the Sixth National Congress under extraordinary circumstances, many of its provisions were inapplicable, and this resulted in the failure of many Party members to pay attention to it and implement it effectively. Therefore, it is incumbent upon the Seventh National Congress to fame a new Party Constitution entirely in conformity with the actual conditions of today.

It is quite clear that our Party now has certain outstanding features which have not existed in any of its previous historical periods. Those features are as follows:

1. Our Party is a party that is national in scale and has a broad mass character. It is a party the people throughout the country are looking up to. With a membership totaling 1,210,000 and with its organizations and members operating in all parts of the country, it is regarded by the whole people as their sole liberator.

2. Our Party is a party that has been steeled in prolonged revolutionary wars and has mastered the art of leading them. The Eighth Route Army, the New Fourth Army and the other armed forces of the people, which have been organized under its leadership constitutes, the main forces present War of Resistance Against Japan. The Chinese nation and people rely on these forces to make post-war China a democratic and united new China.

3. Our is a party that has led the 95 million people living behind the enemy lines in setting up strong revolutionary base areas, where democratic reforms of various forms have been introduced and where new-democratic development in the political, military, economic and cultural fields are under way. These democratic reforms and developments have resulted in increased production, in improvement in the people's living standards, greater social stability and a heightening of the people's cultural level and political conciseness. The Party has mobilized and united all the people in these base areas in vigorously resisting the Japanese aggressors, and this has encouraged the revolutionary struggles of people throughout the country. These base areas are a model of new China, and they guarantee that the whole people of our country will win victory in the revolution.

4. Our Party is a party that has overcome various kinds of erroneous ideas and achieved unprecedented ideological, political and organizational unity and solidarity through a rectification movement. Past opportunist lines have been liquidated and non-proletarian ideas have been largely defeated in the rectification movement,(181) while the proletarian Marxist-Leninist line as

represented by Comrade Mao Zedong have won an un paralleled, solid victory throughout the Party. Many of the saboteurs and spies who were hiding in our Party and trying to undermine the nation have been combed out. Thus, our Party has become united and consolidated ideologically, politically and organizationally as never before. This has contributed immeasurably to the cause of China's liberation.

5. Last, but by no means least, our Party is a party that has a great leader of its own. He is none other than Comrade Mao Zedong, the organizer and leader of our Party and of the present-day Chinese revolution. Comrade Mao Zedong is an outstanding representative of the heroic proletariat of our country and of the fine traditions of our nation. He is a talented and creative Marxist, integrating, as he does, the universal truth of Marxism — the most advanced ideology in the history of mankind — with the concrete practice of the Chinese revolution. He has thus raised the ideology of the Chinese nation to a rational height unknown before and has shown the suffering Chinese nation and people the only correct road leading to complete liberation — the road of Mao Zedong. Following this road, our Party and the Chinese people launched the great pre-1927 revolutionary movement of which he was one of the organizers. During the agrarian revolution in the Soviet areas,(6) the great Red areas and the Red Army were created with Comrade Mao Zedong as their most outstanding founder and leader. In the War of Resistance Against Japan, the great Liberated Areas and the people's armed forces — the Eighth Route Army and the New Fourth Army — were created, and again he was the founder and leader. Comrade Mao Zedong is the

leader of our Party, but he is also an ordinary member of our Party, being completely at the service of the Party and most scrupulous in the observance of Party discipline in every respect. He is the leader of the masses, yet he bases everything on the will of the people. He stands before the people as their most loyal servant and their most modest pupil. Being a figure who has emerged from the revolutionary struggles of the people and who has been tested through more than thirty years of the great Chinese revolutionary struggle, he is well known to the entire Party and the people of the whole country. It is the carefully considered choice of our Party and of the Chinese nation and people that he becomes their leader. Our Party has not only a great leader of its own, but also a large number of well-tried cadres who, rallying round him armed with Mao Zedong Thought, act as the backbone of the Party. These cadres have proved, during a long period of struggle, to be the finest people, the cream of the Chinese nation, and men of action in every field of the Chinese people's revolution and national construction. With such a great leader and with a large group of such cadres, we are invincible and will vanquish all the enemies of the Chinese nation and people.

Comrades, our Party is already a Marxist-Leninist party which is national in scale, has a broad mass character, is fully consolidated ideologically, politically and organizationally and is under a leader of its own. It has now become the determining factor in China's political life.

Such are the main features of our Party today.

Such are the brilliant successes our Party has achieved. They are great victories for the Chinese people as a whole, great victories for Marxism-Leninism among the Chinese people and great victories for the teachings and leadership of Comrade Mao Zedong, the leader of our Party.

However, this does not mean our Party is without any shortcomings or weaknesses. Nor dose it mean that there are no difficulties ahead. We still have shortcomings and weaknesses and, for all our achievements, we are still far from our goal. here are still many difficulties ahead to be overcome. The bulk of our Party is still in the countryside and the overwhelming majority of Party members are of peasant of petty-bourgeois origin. Generally speaking, their theoretical and cultural level is not high, although they have been steeled in fierce revolutionary struggles. Some of our comrades have not yet completely overcome their subjectivist style of work, while others display such tendencies as commandism, bureaucratism and warlordism, which estrange the masses from the Party. Still others have the "mountain-stronghold" mentality which impairs the unity and solidarity of the Party. These shortcomings and weaknesses in our Party can only be overcome through greater efforts and more painstaking education.

Having undergone long, heroic struggles, especially the heroic war of resistance in the last eight years, our Party and the Chinese nation and people are now approaching victory. Our present task is to prepare to seize victory; to mobilize and unite all the forces of the Chinese people, in co-operation with our Allies, for the final expulsion of the Japanese aggressors and the recovery of our lost cities and villages; to conquer the anti-democratic forces throughout the country; and to build an independent, free, democratic, united, prosperous and powerful new China. In order to achieve these objectives we must tremendously improve the work of our Party, strengthen its organizational role and its leadership among all sections of the masses and prepare the people and ourselves ideologically, politically and organizationally for the great struggle and victory, unprecedented in our history. These are the immediate political and organizational tasks of our Party.

The present state of our Party and its tasks constitute the point of departure in our revision of the Party Constitution today.

* * *

This was the Report on the Revision of the Party Constitution delivered at the Seventh National Congress of the Chinese Communist Party held in Yan'an from April 23 to June 11, 1945. In January 1950, it was published by the People's Publishing House under the title, *On the Party* by the author. The book consists of nine sections, of which sections one, two and five are included in this volume.

2. The General Programme of the Party Constitution

We have formulated a General Programme to serve as an introduction to the Constitution. It is the basic programme of our Party. As a component of the Party Constitution, this preamble sets out the general principles of the Party Constitution. Every Party member must accept this General Programme as the basis for all his activities. It will further strengthen the unity and solidarity of the whole Party.

The General Programme sums up the Party's twenty-four years of experience in struggle while drawing while drawing on the best experience of the world-wide working class movement. It is an embodiment of the teachings of Comrade Mao Zedong, the leader of our Party. Its sets forth the concise language the Party's character and theory; the character, motive forces, tasks and special features of the Chinese revolution; the Party's basic principles with respect to the Chinese revolution and the requirements the Party must meet; the need to eliminate opportunism inside the Party; and the importance of self-criticism, the mass line and organizational principles of the Party. All these points are included in the General Programme of the Party Constitution. However, I wish only to expound on the following questions.

1. Concerning the Character of Our Party

The General Programme of the Constitution begins by pointing out that our Party is the organized vanguard of the Chinese working class and the highest form of its class organization. It represents the interests of the Chinese nation and people. At the present stage it is striving for new democracy in China and its ultimate aim is the realization of communism in

China. Is this character of our Party questionable? I think not.

Prior to the founding of our Party in 1921, the Chinese nation and people, led by their distinguished champions, had waged successive, heroic revolutionary struggles against imperialism and feudalism for eighty years. Owing to both international and domestic developments (the former being principally the First World War and the Great October Socialist Revolution in Russia and the latter, increasingly ferocious imperialist aggression and feudal warlord oppression, the people's revolutionary struggles and the rise of the working-class movement following the May 4th Movement of 1919), the Chinese revolutionaries, as represented by Comrade Mao Zedong, turned for the first time from radical revolutionary democracy to proletarian communism, thereby giving birth to the Communist Party of China. Since its birth, our Party has a clear-cut class consciousness, adopted the proletarian stand in leading the Chinese bourgeois-democratic revolution, integrated the universal truth of Marxism-Leninism with the concrete practice of the Chinese working class movement and the Chinese revolution and cultivated the fine style of work characteristic of an advanced proletarian political party. All these factors have given a new aspect to the Chinese revolution. Today, after twenty-four years of practical trials and tests in the most difficult, torturous and exceedingly intricate political struggles, the Party has not only opened up new prospects for victory in the Chinese revolution, but has also accumulated extremely rich experience which, through Comrade Mao Zedong's crystallization and creative work, has raised to a higher plane the integration of the universal truth of Marxism-Leninism with the concrete practice of the Chinese revolution. This shows that our Party has always been, and is especially so today, a party of a completely new type — a proletarian Marxist-Leninist party.

Although the main body of our Party is operating in the countryside and the vast majority of Party members come from the peasantry and petty-bourgeois intelligentsia while only a small percentage are workers, in the aggregate, Party members of proletarian or semi-proletarian (poor peasant) origin constitute the majority. Naturally, this, among other factors, has given rise to a number of serious problems, such as the wide spread manifestation in the Party of the ideology of small producers. Even bourgeois and feudal ideologists have found their way into our Party through the medium of petty-bourgeois elements. Herein lies the social roots of subjectivism, sectarianism, stereotyped Party writing as well as political and organizational opportunism in our Party. However, this state of affairs cannot alter the fact that our Party is a political party of the proletariat.

The proletarian character of our Party is determined by the following factors:

1. It came into existence and developed in the epoch of the great world proletarian revolution by absorbing the best traditions of the world Marxist-Leninist movement and basing itself on the great working-class movement before 1927 and the revolution of 1927. It has maintained constant ties with the Chinese working-class movement.

2. Our Party has developed in strict adherence to the Marxist-Leninist teachings sinified by Comrade Mao Zedong and to the political and organizational line formulated by him. (All those who ran counter to this line have been discredited by history.) The Marxist-Leninist leadership of the Central Committee headed by comrade Mao Zedong enjoys enormous prestige because a large number of cadres — many of whom emerged directly from the working-class movement — have been steeled in prolonged struggle and are armed with Marxist-Leninist and Mao Zedong Thought, they are fully capable of taking up the cause led by the Central Committee and Comrade Mao Zedong.

3. With its proletarian programme and policy, our Party is distinct from any other political party and has, on its own, organized and led the anti-imperialist and anti-feudal new-democratic revolution of the Chinese people. Having made the realization of socialism and communism its ultimate goal, it has enabled the Chinese proletariat to fulfill its tasks in the present bourgeois-democratic revolution to the fullest extent and to exercise its revolutionary leadership over the masses.

4. Every Party member must observe and not contravene the iron proletarian discipline of the Party. Every Party member is required to abide by the Partys Programme and Constitution and to work in a Party organization. The Party preserves and strengthens its proletarian unity ideologically, politically and organizationally at all times. It has cleared out of its ranks all alien elements and opportunists who are incorrigible beyond remoulding.

5. More than twenty years of both civil war and national war have steeled our Party. Hundreds of thousands of Party members have long left their respective occupations behind to plunge themselves into the revolutionary life of a military community and life-and-death struggle. They have undergone rigorous ideological and organizational education and tempering which has enhanced their class consciousness and collective spirit and strengthened their sense of organization and discipline. They have come to understand that, when confronted with the enemy, all Party members share identical interests and must obey the Party's centralized leadership unconditionally. Wavering elements on the other hand,, will keep dropping out of the Party in the

course of serious revolutionary struggles.

6. Marxist-Leninist education will enable Party members of petty-bourgeois origin to undergo a thoroughgoing ideological remoulding to change their former petty-bourgeois character and gain the qualities of advanced fighters of the proletariat.

A party founded, steeled and educated in such a manner is certainly not inferior — to say the very least — to any proletarian party of the capitalist countries.

It is not just the social origin of Party members but our Party's political struggles and political life, its ideological education and its ideological and political leadership that decide things, and the General Programme of the Party and its organizational principles ensure the dominance of of the proletarian ideology and proletarian line. No matter how broadly petty-bourgeois ideology is manifested in the Party, it has no legitimacy and is being constantly corrected through education and the rectification movement. Moreover, this ideology has been shown to be incompatible with the interests of the people in serious practical struggles and has thus become increasingly discredited. The social origin of our Party membership does not determine the character of our Party anymore than the social composition of the of the membership of the Labour parties in certain European countries does. Although the majority of these members come from the working class, these Labour parties do not represent the working class in their countries, nor are they able to perform the tasks of the working class.

In China, a large number of petty-bourgeois revolutionaries have joined our Party, and this is a very good thing. Our Party must not reject them. While it is true that we should pay close attention to recruiting the advanced elements from among the workers, we should, at the same time, draw in numerous advanced elements from all other sections of the labouring people. Only then will it be possible for our Party to become a powerful party with a mass character. The proletariat must constantly replenish its ranks by recruiting members from the petty-bourgeoisie — this is an immutable historical law.

The petty-bourgeoisie and the peasantry are transitional classes which go through a process of disintegration under the capitalist system. Except for a small number of their members who will become members of the bourgeoisie, the majority will go bankrupt and swell the ranks of the proletariat. Being transitional classes, they may accept the political leadership of either the liberal bourgeoisie or the proletariat., and ideologically they may be influenced by either of these groups. Hence, under certain historical conditions, large numbers of revolutionary elements among the petty bourgeoisie may join the proletarian party and be susceptible to proletarian education. The proletarian party, our Party, is capable of educating and remoulding them. Experience shows that after joining our Party on our terms, most are conscientious in their studies, willing to receive the Party's education in Marxism-Leninism and Mao Zedong Thought, observe Party discipline and take part in the practical revolutionary struggles of the people. Consequently, they change their original character and become Marxist-Leninists, fighters for the proletariat, and many have even sacrificed their lives for the Party's cause — the realization of communism in China. However, there is also a very small number, who after joining the Party, fail to study Marxism-Leninism and Mao Zedong Thought earnestly and correctly. Holding on to their old viewpoints or styles of work and sometimes even stubbornly opposing those of the proletariat, they try to reconstruct our Party and rebuild its internal life according to their own petty-bourgeois concepts and tastes. Quite naturally they not only fail to become genuine Marxist-Leninists, fighters for the proletariat, but are also responsible for many mistakes and divergences occurring in the Party. The Party's experience shows that this has happened over and over again.

Therefore, all those who join our Party must seriously study Marxism-Leninism and Mao Zedong Thought. The petty-bourgeois revolutionary elements must, both before and after their admission into the Party be especially studious in order to remould their ideology. They must discard their original class stand to adopt the class stand of the proletariat and mus overcome their subjective, individualistic and sectarian tendencies. They cannot become good Party members without such remoulding. This is generally a long painstaking process which, when they are not fully aware of the need, can even be agonizing for many petty-bourgeois revolutionary elements This remoulding is a particularly important question or aspect in the building of our Party.

Inherent in our Party are the essential contradictions between proletarian ideologies and non-proletarian ideologies. The principal contradiction is between the ideology of the proletariat and the ideology of the peasantry and petty bourgeoisie. Our Party building and the cause of our Party can only advance and develop when we have gradually resolved this contradiction by intensifying our education and training in Marxism-Leninism, which is the scientific ideology of the proletariat and by continually overcoming the petty-bourgeois and other ideologies. reflected in our Party. If, conversely, petty-bourgeois ideology is allowed to spread freely within the Party and if it should come to dominate the Partys leadership and repress the development of proletarian ideas, the development and work of our Party will certainly retrogress and fail. Hence, in our Party building the principal need is for ideological development, that is, remoulding our Party members, especially the petty-bourgeois revolutionary elements, through education in Marxism-Leninism, the scientific ideology of the proletariat. In other words, we need to combat and overcome every kind of non-proletarian ideology in the Party.

Chinas petty bourgeoisie is numerically large and many of our Party members are of petty-bourgeois origin. In the past, both Chinas proletariat and our Party were in their infancy, lacking experience. Our Party did not have sufficient ideological preparation in Marxism-Leninism before its foundation, nor did it have enough time thereafter for theoretical study and propaganda work because it immediately immersed itself in turbulent, practical revolutionary struggle. For these reasons, our Party suffered for a long time form inadequate Marxist-Leninist ideological education. It was, therefore, possible for the petty-bourgeois elements inside our Party who hadnt undergone remoulding to propagate what was in essence opportunism under the cloak of Marxism-Leninism, by taking advantage of the ideological of many Party members and the petty-bourgeois sentiments in the Party. This is how petty-bourgeois ideology gained temporary predominance in the Partys leading bodies at certain periods.

When the petty-bourgeois ideology was predominate in the Party leadership, Right of Left opportunist lines were carried out not only politically but in the building and the organization of the Party.

The right opportunist line in the building and organization of the Party took the form of the liberalist line perused by certain comrades. They attempted to turn our Party into a liberalist party of the petty bourgeoisie. They opposed and discarded the Partys principled stand in ideological and organizational matters. They undermined the Partys democratic centralism and iron discipline by enrolling Party members en masse and without discrimination, allowing all sorts of erroneous ideas to spread within the Party unchecked, abandoning vigilance against the partys enemies and saboteurs and encouraging " showing off", lax discipline and factional tendencies and spontaneity within the Party. It is quite obvious that had these things continued, the result would have been to prevent our Party from accomplishing anything and to bring about its collapse.

The "Left" opportunist line in building and organization of the Party found expression in the action of some comrades who, ignoring Chinas special characteristics, mechanically imported the Party-building experience of Parties abroad and turned them into absolute dogmas. They placed one-sided emphasis on inner-Party centralism and inner-Party struggle, and they admitted no compromise and laid stress on mechanical discipline. They discarded inner-Party democracy and harmony, serious discussion of problems and relevant criticism and paid no heed to the political consciousness and initiative of Party members. Like patriarchs, they issued orders and ruled arbitrarily within the Party. They perused a policy of obscurantism. They encouraged blind obedience on the part of Party members, carried on mercilessly inner-Party struggles and engaged in punitiveness. They punished, expelled or purged Party members wholesale. As a result mechanical discipline and feudalistic order prevailed in the Party and inner-Party life became stagnant. Temporarily this may have created the appearance of inner-Party unity. But such unity was false, superficial and mechanical. Once found out it could have given way to a state of inner-Party anarchy, characteristic of ultra-democracy. It is quite obvious that such a line could destroy our Party by relegating it to a narrow, lifeless, sectarian faction.

These two deviations are reflections of petty-bourgeois liberalism and sectarionism as well as impetuosity on the question of organization.

In addition to the two deviations mentioned above, there were still other comrades who, because of their ideological weakness and political blindness, stressed only the organizational aspect of Party building to the neglect of the ideological and political building of the Party. The result was that Party building became a formality. They favoured and commended those "honest fellows" who were capable of nothing but blind obedience while they feared and blamed those who could do their own thinking, were highly capable and refused to obey blindly. They attached too much importance to the petty trifles in the daily lives of others while ignoring the one task of supreme importance, namely, enlightening and raising the ideological and political consciousness of Party members and thus strengthening the organization and discipline of the Party. Also failing to understand that in order to attain this objective, it is essential first of all to arouse and raise the consciousness of the high and middle-ranking cadres, they gave their minds only to the Party members of worker or peasant origin, and they were afraid of capable intellectuals. They busied themselves with so called organizational "leadership"; holding meetings, running here and there and occupying themselves with all kinds of trifling matters. But they did not use their brains. Instead of improving organizational leadership and linking it with ideological and political leadership, they separated the Partys organizational work from ideological and political leadership. This is blindness in Party building. Quite obviously, this is not the way to build up a Marxist-Leninist proletarian party, because opportunists inside the Party may very well take advantage of such a situation.

Our Party has overcome such erroneous ideas by ceaselessly waging uncompromising struggle against them. It has unanimously supported and followed Comrade Mao Zedongs line of Party building. In sharp contrast to the erroneous lines mentioned above, this correct line of Comrade Mao Zedong first of all lays stress on ideological and political building with out neglecting organizational building. He has repeatedly told us that ideological education and leadership should come first when our Party exercises leadership. He formulated detailed political, military and organizational lines for our Party. In the Revolution of the Gutian Meeting in 1929, he drew attention to the various erroneous deviations originating in non-proletarian ideology inside the Party and called upon our comrades to eliminate them. He also adopted a creative method of education in the form of rectification movement to remove all such petty-bourgeois ideology. He considered the development of our Party a process through which the universal truth of Marxism-Leninism was to be integrated ever more closely with the concrete practice of the

Chinese revolution. He linked the building of the Party closely with the Partys political line, with our partys relationship to the bourgeoisie and to armed struggle. Comrade Mao Zedongs *On Correcting Mistaken Ideas in the Party,* the second part of his *On the New Stage* and his *Introducing "The Communist", Reform Our Study, Rectify the Party's Style of Work, Oppose Stereotyped Party Writing, Decisions by the Central Committee on Continuing the Rectification Movement* (April 3, 1943), *Some Questions Concerning Methods of Leadership* (June 1, 1943) and other works are direct expression of his correct line on Party building, formulated to our Party's special features. The implementation of this line has enabled us to overcome all kinds of opportunist and other erroneous lines in Party building, with the result that the Party has made tremendous progress and achieved great success.

It is clear that had our Party followed these erroneous lines on Party building, it would not have become a party of the working class even if the percentage of workers in our Party membership had been higher. But as we have followed Comrade Mao Zedong's line, we can build, and have already built, a Marxist-Leninist party of the working class, even though the workers in our Party membership do not yet constitute the majority.

For many years the bulk of our Party has been operating in the rural areas because China is a semi-colonial and semi-feudal country and because the peasant masses constitute the main force of the present revolution. In addition, the Chinese working class, being oppressed in the cities and for a long time unable to carry on revolutionary activities freely, has had to send its vanguard to the countryside to organize its vast ally and to act in co-ordination with it to liberate the cities when the conditions become favourable. Here lies the true significance of our Party's long-term work in the countryside. Under circumstances as they exist in this present period, this is the only way our Party can represent the Chinese working class and carry out its tasks. If our Party acts otherwise, it will never represent the Chinese working class because the present revolution in China is essentially a peasant revolution. The basic and immediate task of the Chinese working class is to emancipate the Chinese peasantry. Under the leadership of a proletarian party, the great peasant war differs from all others in Chinese history, and it absolutely can be victorious. It is quite logical, therefore, that over the long years our Party has, as the vanguard of the working class, been organizing and leading this peasant revolution in the countryside with might and main.

The General Programme of the Party Constitution points out that our Party represents the interests of the Chinese nation and people. This is no doubt the essence of our Party and of Mao Zedong Thought. The interests of the Chinese proletariat are at all times identical with those of the Chinese people. The new-democratic revolution now being waged by our Party against imperialism and feudalism is in the interests not just of the working class but of the peasantry, the petty-bourgeoisie and the bourgeoisie, too. The Chinese Communist Party can succeed only when it stands for the interests of the whole people, instead of merely for the partial and immediate interests of one class. The proletariat cannot win its own emancipation if it fails to emancipate the people as a whole. On the other hand, the Chinese working class and the working people as a whole constitute the main body of the Chinese nation. It is their interests that form the foundation of the interests of the Chinese nation and people. In fighting for an independent, free, democratic, united, prosperous and powerful new China, the Chinese Communist Party is representing the interests of the entire Chinese nation and people as well as those of the Chinese working class. The same will be true in the future when it will fight for socialism and communism, because the realization or a socialist and communist society will mean final emancipation of all mankind.

2. Concerning the Guiding Ideology of Our Party

The General Programme of the Party Constitution states that the Chinese Communist Party is guided in all its work by Mao Zedong Thought — the doctrine that integrates the theory of Marxism-Leninism with the practice of the Chinese revolution — and that it is opposed to any dogmatic or empiricist deviations. As for our Chinese and foreign heritage, we neither reject it nor accept it without discrimination; we accept critically what is valuable and appropriate and repudiate what is erroneous and inappropriate, basing our judgement on Marxist dialectical materialism and historical materialism. All this is made very clear.

The General Programme of the Party Constitution provides that Mao Zedong Thought shall guide the work of our Party. The Constitution also states that it is the duty of every Party member to endeavour to learn the fundamentals of Marxism-Leninism and Mao Zedong Thought. This is a most important historical characteristic of our present revision of the Constitution. I believe that this Congress and the entire Party membership will heartily support this provision.

For over a century the Chinese nation and people have suffered incredible hardships. They have accumulated rich experience in the struggles for their own emancipation, in which much blood has been shed. Their practical struggles and experience inevitably gave rise to a great body of theory demonstrating that the Chinese people are not only good at fighting but also capable of arming themselves with modern scientific revolutionary theory. Because of the political and economic flabbiness of China's bourgeoisie and because of its lack of contact with the people and its limited outlook and thinking, its representatives could only advance certain revolutionary programmes and democratic ideas. We have already adopted all the good points of their programmes and ideas as part of our heritage. The representatives could not, however, formulate a systematic revolutionary theory, much less a comprehensive, systematic and scientific theory in relation to the whole course of Chinese history and the Chinese revolution. Such a theory can only be created by the representatives of the Chinese proletariat, of whom the greatest and most outstanding is Comrade Mao Zedong.

Our Congress should warmly celebrate the development of a unique, integrated and correct theory of the peoples revolution and national reconstruction which has been maturing since the founding of the Chinese Communist Party. This theory has led our Party and our people to great victories and it will lead us to ultimate and complete victory and emancipation. It is the greatest achievement and glory of the Party and the Chinese people in their long struggles and will benefit our nation for generation upon generation. This theory is none other than Mao Zedong Thought — Comrade Mao Zedong's theories with regard to Chinese history, Chinese society and the Chinese revolution and relevant policies.

Mao Zedong Thought is the theory which integrates Marxist-Leninist theories with the practice of the Chinese revolution. It is communism and Marxism applied to China.

Mao Zedong Thought is the development of Marxism with regard to the national-democratic revolution in the colonial, semi-colonial and semi-feudal country of the present period. It is an outstanding example of how Marxism is applied to a given nation. It has taken shape and has developed in the course of the long revolutionary struggles of the Chinese nation and people which include the three great revolutionary wars (the Northern Expedition, (120) the Agrarian Revolutionary War and the present War of Resistance Against Japan). It is at once Chinese and thoroughly Marxist. It has evolved through the application of the Marxist world outlook and social outlook, specifically, dialectical materialism and historical materialism. In other words, it has evolved it has evolved through careful, scientific analysis of the exceedingly rich experience of all modern revolutions. This includes of course, the experience gained by the Chinese Communist Party in directing the revolutionary struggle of the Chinese people in the light of the characteristics of the Chinese nation and on the solid foundation of Marxist-Leninist theories. As theories and politics for achieving the emancipation of the Chinese nation and people, Mao Zedong Thought has developed by applying the scientific method of Marxism-Leninism to a synthesis of China's history, social conditions and entire revolutionary experience with a view to furthering the interests of the proletariat and consequently the entire people. These are therefore, the only correct theories and policies with which the proletariat and all working people of China fight for their emancipation.

Mao Zedong Thought — the theory and practice of communism applied to China — has come into being and developed not only in the course of the revolutionary struggles against domestic and foreign enemies but also in the course of the principled struggles against various erroneous opportunist ideas within the Party, such as, Chen Duxiuism,(110) the Li Lisan line (18) and the subsequent "Left" deviationist line, capitulationist line, dogmatism and empiricism. It is our Party's only correct guiding ideology and its only correct general line.

In the twenty-four years since its birth, Mao Zedong Thought has developed and matured. It has stood the test of innumerable bitter struggles of millions upon millions of people and has been proved to be objective truth and embody the only correct theories and policies for saving China. Numerous historical events have borne out the fact that whenever the revolution follows the leadership of Comrade Mao Zedong and Mao Zedong Thought, it will go forward and succeed and whenever it departs from that leadership, it will go down-hill and eventually fail. The integration of Marxist theory with both the practice of the proletarian revolution in the era of imperialism and the practice of the Russian revolution gave rise to Russian Bolshevism (16) — Leninism. Leninism has not only led the Russian people to complete emancipation but also guided and still is guiding the people of the whole world in their

31

struggle for emancipation.. As a pupil of Marx, Engels, Lenin and Stalin, Comrade Mao Zedong has exactly effected the integration of the Marxist-Leninist theories with the practice of the Chinese revolution. This has given rise to Chinese communism — Mao Zedong Thought — which has guided, and is still guiding, the Chinese people towards complete emancipation and which has made useful contribution to the cause of emancipation of the people all over the world, particularly people in the East.

Mao Zedong Thought, in terms of world outlook and style of work, is Marxism being developed and improved through its application in China. It constitutes the comprehensive theories of revolution and national reconstruction for the Chinese people. These theories are to be found in Comrade Mao Zedong's writings and in many works of our Party literature. They include Comrade Mao Zedong's analysis of the present world situation and Chinas conditions and his theories and policies with regard to New Democracy, the emancipation of the peasantry, the revolutionary united front, revolutionary wars, revolutionary bases, the establishment of a new-democratic republic, Party building, culture, etc. These theories and policies are at once thoroughly Marxist and thoroughly Chinese. They are the highest expression of the wisdom of the Chinese people and the most succinct of theoretical generalizations.

Because of the distinctive characteristics of China's social and historical development and its backwardness in science, it is a unique and herculean task to apply Marxism systematically to China, to transform it from its European form into a Chinese form and thereby to solve the various problems in the contemporary Chinese revolution from the Marxist standpoint and with the Marxist method. Many of our problems have never been considered or approached by the worlds Marxists because, unlike the conditions in other countries, in China the main sections of the masses are not workers but peasants and the fight is directed not against domestic capitalism but against foreign imperialist oppression and feudal practices. This can never be accomplished, as some people seem to think it can, by memorizing and reciting Marxist works or by just quoting from them. It requires a high level of the combination of scientific and revolutionary spirit. It requires profound historical and social knowledge, rich experience in guiding the revolutionary struggles and skill in using Marxist-Leninist methods to make an accurate, scientific analysis of social and historical conditions and their development. It further requires boundless and tenacious loyalty to the cause of the proletariat and the people, faith in the strength, creative power and future of the masses and skill in crystallizing the experience, ideas and will of the masses and in bringing what is crystallized back to the masses for application. Only thus is it possible to make original and brilliant additions to Marxism-Leninism in the light of the historical development of each specific period and the concrete economic and political conditions in China, to express Marxism-Leninism in plain language easily understood by the Chinese people, to adapt it to the new historical environment and Chinas special conditions and to make it a weapon in the hands of the Chinese proletariat and the working people. No one but our Comrade Mao Zedong has so splendidly and successfully performed the extremely difficult task of adapting Marxism to China. This constitutes one of the greatest achievements in the history of the Marxist movement all over the world, and the dissemination of Marxism — the best of all truths — in a nation of 475 million people is unprecedented. This is something for which we should be particularly grateful.

Our Comrade Mao Zedong is not only the greatest revolutionary and statesman in Chinese history, but also the greatest theoretician and scientist. He has had the prowess to lead the whole Party and the entire Chinese people to wage struggles that shook the world and, what is more, he has been the best-versed and sternest challenger to theories. In the theoretical field, he has been bold in blazing the trail. He has discarded certain Marxist principles and conclusions that are outmoded or incompatible with the concrete conditions in China and replaced them with appropriate new ones. For this reason he has been able to successfully carry out the difficult and monumental task of sinifying Marxism.

Because of inadequate theoretical preparation, our Party and many Party members have been confused about how to do their work and so have suffered a lot, making quite a few unnecessary detours. Now, thanks to Comrade Mao Zedongs painstaking work and brilliant creativity, the groundwork has been fully laid for our Party and the Chinese people. This will greatly enhance our self-confidence and our ability to fight and speed the Chinese revolution to victory. Therefore, the important task now is to mobilize the entire Party membership to study and disseminate Mao Zedong Thought and to arm our membership and revolutionary people with it, so that it may become a living, irresistible force. For this purpose, all Party schools and training classes must adopt Comrade Mao Zedongs writings as basic teaching material, and the cadres must study these writings systematically. Our entire Party press must propagate Mao Zedong Thought in a systematic way. The propaganda departments of the Party should edit Comrade Mao Zedongs important works into popular reading matter suited to the level of the average Party member.

After having overcome thought-stifling dogmatism in the Party, we must make further efforts to remove the obstacle of empiricism and to start a campaign in the Party to study Mao Zedong Thought. We may then anticipate a great upsurge in the Party of Marxist culture which is ideological preparation for the victory of the peoples revolution in China.

Mao Zedong Thought is the foundation of the present revised Party Constitution and its General Programme. It is the duty of all Party members to study it, to disseminate it and follow its guidance in their work.

3. Concerning the Characteristics of the Chinese Revolution

The General Programme of the Party Constitution points out that present-day Chinese society is semi-feudal in nature. But the Liberated Areas, with a total population approaching 100 million, are of a new-democratic character. This demonstrates the economic and political unevenness and complexity of Chinese society.

The nature of the Chinese society, the fact that the basic motive forces of the Chinese revolution is the proletarian-led masses who's main force is the peasantry, the existence of the powerful Chinese Communist Party and the prevailing international situation are all factors which have come together to determine that Chinese revolution can be neither a bourgeois-democratic revolution of the old type nor a proletarian-socialist revolution of the newest type, but that it must be a bourgeois-democratic revolution of a new type. In this revolution, though the basic motive forces are the proletariat, the peasantry and the petty bourgeoisie, other classes may join the revolution, and we also have numerous allies both at home and abroad. Therefore, the task of the Chinese Communist Party at the present stage is to unite all classes, strata, nationalities and individuals that may take part in the revolution to fight for the complete elimination of oppression by both foreign imperialism and domestic feudalism and to fight for the establishment of a new-democratic republic of China based on an alliance of all revolutionary classes and the voluntary alliance of all nationalities. Only after this revolution has been completed, only when China's economy has developed to its full extent in a new-democratic country, only when many necessary preparatory steps have been taken and, finally, only when the Chinese people feel the need and desire for it, can a socialist and communist system be set up in China. This question, on which there has been some confusion and much debate in the Party in the past, has now been defiantly clarified.

The General Programme of the Party Constitution also deals with many other special characteristics of the Chinese revolution These include the uneven development of the revolution and consequently its protracted nature and complexity, and the importance at given periods of armed struggle and revolutionary bases in the rural areas. All these points have been clarified.

The special characteristics of the Chinese revolution used to be the most contraversial issue within the Party. Opportunists have invariably been mistaken on this question. It is in the course of struggle against opportunism on this issue that Mao Zedong Thought has attained its full development. Hence, there is the need to explain and affirm these characteristics in the General Programme of the Party Constitution. It is necessary for every Party member to aquire a profound understanding of them.

The best explanation of the specila characteristics of the Chinese revolution is to be found in the history of our Party. Traversing a glorious, unique and historical path and coming to grips with and giving play to the special characteristics of our revolution, our Parter has grown under the guidence of Mao Zedong Thought, from a small group of Marxists(193) formed after the May 4th Movement of 1919 to its position today leading strong revolutionary base areas.

The Chinese Communist Party has developed on the basis of the workers' movement and the Chinese people's struggle for emancipation, and it has developed in the course of the revolutionary struggle against national oppression by foreign imperialism and against oppression of the masses by domestic feudalism. It has grown in the course of these revolutionary struggles against all the enemies of the Chinese nation and people. The history of our Party is the history of the

36

Chinese working class uniting with and leading the people in revolutionary struggle against foreign imperialism, which oppressed the whole nation, against domestic feudalism, which oppressed the people and against the lackeys and hidden agents of both.

The Chinese Communist Party has developed and tempered itself in three great revolutionary wars — the Northern Expedition, the Agrarian Revolutionary War and the War of Resistance Against Japan. In other words, it has developed and tempered itself in the course of protracted armed struggle. For many years the history of our Party has been a history of these three revolutionary wars.

The Chinese Communist Party has matured during the course of promoting its unity with the broad masses of peasants and the urban petty bourgeoisie. It has also mathured through unitting with the bourgeoisie against common foes, though it has had to conduct many-sided struggles against the comprimising, reactionarty character of the bourgeoisie. The history of our Party is, therefore, a history of close unity with the broad masses of peasents and the urban petty bourgeoisie and of both unity and struggle vis-à-vis the bourgeoisie.

The Chinese Communist Party has grown up in the course of building great revolutionary base areas, particularly those in the countryside, and in the course of carrying out new-democratic political, military, economic and cultural reforms and construction oin these base areas. For many years the history of our Party has been a history of building base areas for the contempory Chinese revolution, particularly those in the countryside, and of successfully expeerimenting with different kinds of new-democratic reforms and constructions in these areas, which helped to educate our Party and the people throiughout the country.

Lastly, the Chinese Communist Party, as represented by Comrade Mao Zedong, has developed and consolidated itself throught its struggles against the opportunists who ignored or misunderstood the special characteristics of the Chinese revolution, against the dogmatism and empiricism, against Chen Duxiuism and the Li Lisan line and against the subsequent 'Left' line and capitulationism. It hase done so by integrating the universal truth of Marxism-Leninism ever more closely with the practice of the Chinese revolution. The history of our Party is a history of opposing and crushing opportunism of all discriptions and of continuous intigration of the universal truth of Marxism-Leninism with the concrete practice of the Chinese revolution.

All this constitutes the concrete historical road our Party has traversed.

This historical road provides the best expalnation of the character and motive forces of the present Chinese revolution, its uneven development and, consequently, its protracted nature, the complexity of the revolutionary struggle and the importance of armed struggle and of the rural revolutionary base areas. It shows that the development of the Chinese revolution has its own special features. It points to the decisive role which the Marxist-Leninist leadership of the proletariat is playing in this revolution.

The histroical rode our Party has traversed is one which Comrade Mao Zedong, the leader of our Party defined long ago on the basis of the characteristics of the Chinese revolution. The road he has shown us reflects most correctly and fully the course of our Party's history and the course of the contempory revolution of the Chinese nation and people. At certain historical periods he was not in a position to determine the action of the entire Party through formal, organization chanels, and it is precicely these histroical periods that best demonstrate that the true fate of our Party and the correct revolutionary orientation of the Chinese proletariat and people lay with, and continued to be developed by Comrade Mao Zedong. He alone is the people's representative and nucleus.

Our Party, guided by Mao Zedong Thought, has

38

developed and tempered itself in the long course of the Chinese revolution, which has special characteristics. In the years to come it will continue to do so in the course of fighting for its goal under the guidance of Mao Zedong Thought and in the course of acquiring a more profound understanding of and making better use of its special characteristics. For this reason, in the General Programme of the Party Constitution, special emphasis is layed on these characteristics, which will exist until a complete and nationwide victory is won. in China's new-democratic revolution. Therefore, every Party member must constantly bear them in mind and must not for a moment forget them in order to avoid or minimize mistakes in his work. Otherwise, many of the msitakes in hte past may be repeated. For instance, failure failure to understand the extreme uneveness of the Chinese revolution and the resultant complexity of the revolutionary struggles has given rise to over-centralization, unnecessary regimentation, over-simplification, generalization and lack of flexibility in our work. Failure to understand the protracted nature of the Chinese revolution and the lack of adequate mental preparation for the long-drawn-out and difficult struglles has given rise to various forms of impetuosity or pessimism in difficult times. Failure to understand the importance of armed struggle in the Chinese revolution has led to the msitake of undereestimating army work and neglecting the acquisition of military knowledge. Failure to appreciate the importance of rural revolutionary base areas has resulted in the mistake of imposing the urban point of view nu rural circumstances and neglecting rural work. Likewise, failure to appreciate the importance of urban work at certain periods has led to the mistake of neglecting it and clinging to rural conservatism. Failure to realize the necessity of carrying on long-term and patient work among all sections of the people has led to putschism, adventurism and commandism, and so on and so forth. For our comrades to understand these characteristics merely in a general sense is quite inadequate. They must take them into account in their work and in dealing with every specific issue if they are to avoid or minimize mistakes. These characteristics shoulkd therefore be, atleast for the present stage, taken as part of our Party's fundamental programme.

4. Concerning the Mass Line of our Party

Another feature of the present revised Constitution is that particular stress has been alid on the Party's mass line in the General Programme and in the detaioled provisions of the Party Constitution, because the mass line is the fundamental political and organizational line of our Party. This means that all our Party organizations and Pary work must be closely linked with the masses.

Comrade Mao Zedong has repedtedly pointed out to us that the mass line should be applied in all our work. In his report to this Congress, he again urged us in most sincere terms to carry out our work in accordance with the mass line. He said that one hallmark distinguishing our Party from all other political parties was that we have very close ties with the broadest masses of the people. He asked us "to serve the people whole-heartedly and never for a moment divorce ourselves from the masses, to proceed in all cases from the interests of the people and not from the interests of individual groups".(194) He wanted our comrades to understand that " the supreme test of the words and deeds of a Communist is whether they conform with the highest interests and enjoy the support of the overwhelming majority of the people".(195) He further told us that we would be invincible "as loing as we rely on the people, believe firmly in the inexhaustable creative power of the masses and hence trust and identify ourselves with them".(196) He pointed out that "commandism is wrong in any type of work, because in overstepping the level of political consciousness of the masses and violating the principle of voluntary mass action it reflects the disease of impetuosity". And he added, "Tailism in any type of work is also wrong, because it is falling below the level of political consciousness of the masses and violating the principle of leading the masses forward it reflects the disease of dilatoriness."(197) All these teachings of Comrade Mao Zedong are extremly improtant, and every Party member should carefully study and grasp them and esrnestly carry them out.

This mass line of ours is possible only in a proletarian party. It is a class line — the mass line of the proleteriat. Our view of the masses and our relationship with them are diametracally opposed to those of the exploiting classes.

We fully understand the decisive role which the vanguard of the masses can play throughout the people's struggle for emancipation. The complete emancipation of the people is possible only when they have a vanguard of their own, such as our Party. Otherwise they would be without revolutionary leadership, and the people's revolution would consequently meet with failure. Only under the firm and correct leadership of our Party and only by carrying on the struggle along the political orientation given by our Party can the Chinese people achieve their complete emancipation.

This is one aspect of the question.

The other aspect is that the vanguard of the masses must establish proper and close relations wiht the masses. It must stand for the people's interests in all fields, above all in the political field and it must adopt a correct attitude towards the people and lead them by correct methods befroe it can forge close links with them. Otherwise, it is fully possible for the vanguard to become divorced form the people. In that case, it will no longer be the vanguard of the people, and it will not only fail to perform the task of emancipatin the people, but will also face the danger of outright destruction by the enemy. This means that the vanguard of the masses must follow a thorough-going and clear-cut mass line in all its work.

Under what conditions will the vanguard become divorced form the masses?

First of all, the vanguard will divorce itself from the

masses when it fails to perform its obligations as the vanguard of the people, when it fails to represent at all times and in all circumstances the maximum interests of the broadest possible sections of the people, when it fails to define correct tasks, policies and methods of work at the right time and when it fails to stick to the truth and correct its mistakes in good time. In other words, tailism and negligence willl lead to our estrangement from the masses.

In our Party, there has not been any open advocacy or spontaneaty nor has any tailist "theory" been put forward advocating following at the heals of the spontaneous mass movements or dispensing with the leadership of the proletarian party. But Chen Duxiuism in the latter period of the 1924-27 Revolution and capitulationsim in the early period of the War of Resistance Against Japan were both a kind of tailism since their protagonsits laged far behind the mass revolutionary movement of the time. They were incapable of setting forth correct tasks, policies of methods of work to represent the people or inspire them to go forward. Thus they alienated themselves from the people and brought damage or defeat to the revolution. In addition, some comrades have committed errors of a tailist nature in various fields of our work For insance, in their practical work some regarded the Party an apendage to the army, to the leading Party groups in the government, or to the trade unions, instead of the highest form of class organization. Others were lackadaisical, complacent or so bogged down that they just let things drift along and had no desire at all to make improvements. They failed to set forth, based on the prevailing local conditions, correct tasks, policies and methods of work with which to lead the people forward thereby violating the principle of leading the masses step by step. They yielded to the backward ideas of the masses and recuced themselves to the level of ordinary workers, peasants of even backward elements, thus abandoning their vanguard role. At times they gave way to the erroneous ideas of the masses, followed at the tail of spontaneous mass movements and, as a result, failed to give the masses correct and far-sighted leadership This kind of dendancy necessarily isolates us from the broad masses; they do not need such people to lead them.

Secondly, the vanguard divroces itself from the masses when it fails to adopt a correct attitude and correct methods to lead them, when it fails to help them recognize in their own experience the correctness of the Partys slogans and act accordingly, when the slogans it adopts are too radical and the policies ultra-Left, or when the forms of struggle and organization it advocated are impossible to carry out at the time or unacceptable to the masses. In other words, commandism, adventurism and closed-doorism will lead to isolation from the masses.

Some Comrades made the mistake of engaging in commandism, adventurism and cloosed-doorism. Some of them, for instance, were not responsable to the masses in their work. They did not believe that the masses must emancipate themselves through their own efforts. Instead, they stood above and ordered the masses about in order to fight in their stead and to bestow emancipation upon them. Such comrades were impetious so that while they apperared active, in fact they did not know how to transform the Party's slogans and tasks into those of the people. Nor did they know how to elighten the masses or patiently await their awakening, nor did they know how to take steps to help the masses become revolutionary of their own accord. Rather, they tried to compel the masses to accept the Party's slogans and tasks simply by issuing arbitrary orders and forcing the masses into action. Thus they violated the principal volition on the part of the masses. And, especially when the masses harboured misgivings about their radical slogans and ultra-Left policies and felt dissatisfied, they pushed all the harder for their implementation by issuing orders, by coercion or even by threat of punishment. An extreme example of this is the way some of them attempted to frighten the people and cadres into getting the work done by finding mistakes, shortcomings and bad examples whereever they went and by criticizing, condeming and punishing those involved. They did not try to find the strong points or to hold up the good examples, in order to study, develop and systematize them. They did not try to inspire the Party members and the people to go forward and help to overcome the mistakes and shortcomings by commending heroes and model workers or disseminating useful experience. Lashing out in all directions, they tried to get things done by simply issuing orders. Instead of learning from the masses and benefitting from the peoples new ideas and suggestions, they tried to force everyone to do things their way. This tendency led to serious isolation from the masses and aroused resentment not only against the individual comrades but against the Party as well.

In addition to the two tendencies mentioned above, bureaucratism and warlordism have been found among some of our comrades. Tese tenedncies also lead to serious isolation from the masses.

The tendency to bureaucratism is manifested in the fact that some comrades lack the spirit to serve the people and to be responable to the people and the Party. Some typical examples are the way they loaf about all day long, never using their brains; issue orders without without conducting investigation and study of learning from the masses; reject criticism from the masses, ignore their rights or even demand that the people serve them; seek their own benefit at the expense of the interests of the people, not scruppeling to waste public money and man-power; and become corrupt and degenerate and lord it over the people.

The tendency to warlordism is manifested in the fact that some comrades, failing to understand that our army — as the armed force of the people — is a most important instrument of the people for defeating their enemies and winning their liberation, look on the army as a special force standing beyond or above the people, or even as the means of building up their personal influence or position. Consequently, they resort to bureaucratism and commandism in the people's army. They are most conspiciously manifested in the relations between officers and men and between superiors and subordinates. The troops and subordinates are commanded merely through the issuing of orders and the threat of punishment, not through relying on their initiative and consciousness. Secondly, these tendancies are manifested in the relations between the army and the people. In relations with the people some comrades do not try to enforce strict discipline among their subordinates and, instead of cherishing the people, coerce, beat and swear at them. As a result the troops become alienated from the people. Thirdly, these tendencies are mainfested in the purly military approach to the relationship between the revolutionary army and the revolutionary government; that is, it places it palces the army above the government and puts the government under army control as the warlords used to do. Obviously, this tendency is incomparable with the character of a people's army.

These erroneous tendencies in our Party, which alienate us from the masse, arise from the low educational level of the working people and the influence of the exploiting classes of the old society. The petty-bourgeois elements and the other elements in our Party who have long been disengaged from production have generally been susceptible to such influences and tend to divorce themselves from the masses. These tendencies are deep-rooted in society, and we have felt necessary to mention them in the General Programme of our Party Constitution. The more the revolution develops and the more onerous our work becomes, the more likely it is that such tendencies among us will grow. We must, therefore, wage a constant struggle against them in order to maintain and cement our ties with the broad masses of the people. As comrade Mao Zedong puts it, we must constantly "sweep the floor and wash our faces" so as to prevent political dust and germs from clouding the minds of our comrades and decaying the body of our Party.

The masses must have their own staunch vanguard

which, for its part, must maintain close ties with the widest possible section of the masses. Only thus will the emancipation of the people be possible. Our Party, the vanguard of the Chinese people, must constantly try to eradicate tendencies such as those described above which estrange it from the masses, so that we can follow a line of close unity with them. This is the mass line of our Party — the mass line set forth by Comrade Mao Zedong. It is a line designed to enable our Party to establish correct relationship with the people and to adopt a correct attitude and correct methods for leading them. This line will enable our Party's leading organs and individuals to establish a correct relationship with their followers.

According to Comrade Mao Zedong, our Party's policies and methods of work must be "from the masses and to the masses". That is to say, the organizational as well as the political line of our Party should stem genuinely from the masses and be genuinely relayed back to them. Our Partys correct political line cannot be separated from its correct organizational line. Although partial, temporary disharmony may occur between these two, it is impossible to imagine a correct political line existing along side an incorrect organizational line or vice versa The one cannot be isolated from the other. By a correct organizational line we mean the Party's mass line, which calls for closely linking the Party's leading cadres with the rank an file inside and outside the Party, for the principle of "from the masses and to the masses" and for supplementing the general call with specific guidance through leadership.

For the implementation of the mass line of our Party and of Comrade Mao Zedong, the General Programme and provisions of the Party Constitution has laid emphasis on certain viewpoints concerning the masses. Those viewpoints, which every Party member should bear in mind, are as follows:

The first is the viewpoint of doing everything in the interests of the people and of serving them whole-heartedly.

From the outset, our Party our Party was founded to serve the people. All the sacrifices, efforts and struggles of our Party members have been made for no other purpose than the welfare and emancipation of the people. Here lies our greatest glory as Communists, the thing we are most proud of. Therefore any viewpoint that stands for personal interests of the interests of small groups at the expense of those of the people is wrong. So long as they are devoted to their duty and have some achievements to their credit, all our Party members and all those who have joined our ranks are serving the people and putting themselves at their disposal no matter whether they are aware of it or not, or whether they occupy important, leading positions or are ordinary fighters, cooks or grooms. They are all directly or indirectly serving the people at their different posts. Therefore, they are all equal and honourable. We must enhance the political consciousness of all our Party members and personnel so that they may serve the people and hold themselves responsible to the people.

The second is the viewpoint of holding oneself fully responsible to the people. In serving the people, we must we must hold ourselves responsible to them to that they will benefit by our effort and win emancipation. We must try our best to avoid mistakes or reduce them to a minimum in order not to harm the people or cause them losses. To benefit the people, the tasks, policies and methods of work we adopt must all be correct. If they are not correct, they will adversely affect the peoples interests. Should this happen, we must make earnest self-criticism and ensure prompt rectification. This means that we must know how to serve the people and that we must serve them well and not otherwise. Under no circumstances should we adopt a reckless attitude towards the people; we must adopt a serious and responsible attitude.

It is also necessary to understand that being responsible to the people is identical with being responsible to the leading bodies of the Party. This means that although our Party members will be responsible to a leading organ or an individual leader in carrying out its of his instructions, they will err if they separate responsibility to the Party leadership from that to the people. Only by holding oneself responsible to the people can one be considered to have done one's best and utmost. It must be understood that the interests of the Party are identical with those of the people. That which benefits , benefits the Party, and every Party member must work for all such things with might and main. Likewise, what ever harms the people harms the Party and must be opposed or avoided by every Party member. The interests of the people are the interests of the Party. Apart from the interests of the people, the Party has no special interests of its own. The ultimate interests of the greatest number of people is the highest criterion of truth, and consequently, the highest criterion of all the activities of our Party members. A Party member who is responsible to the people is responsible to the Party. It must be understood that responsibility to the Party and responsibility to the people are identical. They should be integrated and must not be separated or set against each other. When short-comings or mistakes are found in the directives of leading organs or individual leaders with regard to tasks, policies or methods of work, suggestions for their correction should be made with a sense of responsibility to the people. We must not be indifferent about what is right and what is wrong; to be so means acting irresponsibly both to the people and to the Party. The basic interests of the Chinese people demand that Party discipline be observed and Party unity maintained. Party discipline and unity must not be undermined on the pretext of being responsible to the people. Nevertheless, any shortcoming or mistake made by a leading body or individual must be corrected. It is the duty as well as the right of every Party member to help in this respect, for any such shortcomings or mistakes are harmful to the people and so also to the Party. Sincere criticism of one's own mistakes and those of the leadership and observance of Party discipline constitute the spirit of responsibility to the people.

The third is the viewpoint of believing in the self-emancipation of the people. Comrade Mao Zedong has pointed out more than once that the people are truly great, that their creative power is inexhaustible, that we are invincible only when we rely on them, that the people alone are the true makers of history and that genuine history is the history of the people. Marx pointed out long ago that the toilers will emancipate themselves,(142) and *The Internationale* states that their salvation depends not upon emperors, gods, or heroes but upon themselves. This means that only through their own struggles and efforts can the people win their emancipation, maintain it and consolidate it. It cannot be bestowed or granted, nor can it be fought for or secured by anybody on their behalf. Hence, any attitude of gratuitously bestowing emancipation on the masses or carrying out their fight for them is wrong.

The people make their own history. Their emancipation must be based on their own consciousness and willingness. They select their vanguard, and under its leadership they get themselves organized and fight for their own emancipation. Only thus can they make conscious efforts to secure, retain and consolidate the fruits of their struggles. The enemies of the people can be overthrown only by the people themselves. It cannot be done in any other way. Without their own genuine consciousness and mobilization, the efforts of their vanguard alone will not suffice for the people to win emancipation, to make progress or to accomplish anything. Even tasks which concern the immediate interests of the people such as the reduction of rent and interest,(139) or the formation of labour-exchange teams and co-operatives will result in pseudo-reduction or formal, empty things, unless, instead of being bestowed on them or organized for them by other people, these tasks are taken up voluntarily and consciously by the masses themselves.

The cause of the Communists is the cause of the people. No matter how correct our programme and policies may be, they cannot be put into effect without the direct support and sustained struggle of the people. With us, therefore, unless everything is dependent on and determined by the people's political consciousness and willingness to act, we can accomplish nothing and all our efforts will be to no avail. With our reliance upon their political consciousness and willingness to act, with their genuine awakening and mobilization and with the Party's correct leadership, we will assuredly win final victory in all aspects of the great cause of our Party. Hence, when the masses are not fully awakened, the duty of Communists, the vanguard of the people, in carrying out any kind of work is to develop their consciousness by every effective and suitable means. This is the first step in our work and it must be done well however difficult and time-consuming it may be. Only when the first step has been taken can we start on the second step. In other words, when the masses have reached the necessary level of consciousness, it is our duty to guide them in their actions — to guide them to organize and to fight. When this has been accomplished, we may, in the course of their actions try to enhance their consciousness a step further. This is how we lead the masses step by step to fight for their basic slogans as put forward by our Party. We Communists and the advanced elements and outstanding figures among the masses can do no more than this for the people's cause And nothing more than this can be expected. Whoever attempts to go beyond this point is liable to commit all kinds of errors, including individualistic heroism, commandism monopolization of affairs and the favour-bestowing viewpoint.

In the struggle for the emancipation of the people, a Communist should act and, indeed, can only act as a leader or guide to them. He should not and cannot possibly act as a "hero" taking for himself the role of conquering the world. In their revolutionary struggle the people are in dire need of far-sighted and staunch leaders and guides and such persons are in fact a prerequisite for the people's success. But the people do not need "heroes" to conquer the world for them, because such "heroes", isolated as they are from the masses, can achieve nothing for the cause of emancipating the people.

The fourth is the viewpoint of learning from the people. In order to serve the people well, to kindle their consciousness and to guide their actions, we Communists must first of all possess certain qualifications such as foresight and the ability to anticipate various problems. This means we must be harbingers, for only such people are capable of helping to enlighten others. In addition to our whole-hearted devotion to the cause of the people's emancipation, our inexhaustible enthusiasm and our sprit of sacrifice, we must acquire adequate knowledge, experience and vigilance before we can successfully raise the people's consciousness, guide their actions and serve them well. Study is indispensable if we are to acquire knowledge, experience and foresight. We can enrich our knowledge by studying Marxist-Leninist theories, our own history and the lessons of the people's struggles in foreign lands. We can also expand our knowledge by learning from our enemies. Most importantly, however, we must learn from the masses, because their knowledge and experience are the most abundant and practical and their creative power is the greatest. This is why Comrade Mao Zedong has time and time again asked us to learn from the masses before we attempt to educate them. Only when our comrades have learned from the masses with an open mind and have crystallized the knowledge and experience of the people into a system of knowledge of a higher order, will they be able to take specific steps to develop the consciousness of the people and give guidance to their activities. If, instead of learning from the masses, we think ourselves clever and try to develop the consciousness of the masses and guide them by devising a set of schemes out of our own imagination or mechanically introducing a set of schemes based on historical or foreign experiences, the attempt will certainly prove futile. In order to keep on learning from the masses, we must not stand apart from them for a single moment. If we isolate ourselves from them, our knowledge will be extremely limited and we will certainly not be clever, well-informed, capable or competent enough to give them leadership.

"Simple people sometimes prove to be much nearer to the truth than some high institutions.

"Our experience alone. the experience of the leaders, is far from enough for the leadership of our cause. In order to lead properly the experience of the leaders must be supplemented by the experience of the Party membership, the experience of the working class,, the experience of the toilers, the experience of the so-called 'little people.'

"It is possible to do that only when the leaders are most closely connected with the masses, when they are connected with the Party membership, with the working class, with the peasantry, with the working intelligentsia.

"Connection with the masses, strengthening this connection,, readiness to head the voice of the masses — herein lies the strength and invincibility of the Bolshevik leadership."(198)

Such is Stalin's advice to the Communists of the Soviet Union. It is a universal truth.

The task of the leaders and the leading bodies is to exercise correct leadership, size up the situation correctly, grasp its essence, set forth the tasks, make decisions, mobilize and organize the masses to implement these decisions and supervise the work of implementation. To do this well it is essential to learn from the masses and to follow the line of "from the masses to the masses"; otherwise no leadership can be satisfactorily exercised.

This is what the viewpoint of learning from the masses means.

The viewpoints of doing everything in the interests of the people, of holding oneself fully responsible to them, of believing in their self-emancipation and of learning from them to constitute our mass viewpoints, which are the viewpoints of the vanguard of the people. Only with such viewpoints, the firm and unequivocal mass view points, can our comrades follow a clear-cut mass line in their work and exercise correct leadership.

our comrades follow a clear-cut mass line in their work and exercise correct leadership.

Some comrades consider mass work to be, to the exclusion of other kinds, only the work of such mass organizations as trade unions or peasant associations. This is wrong. All Party activities and all activities under the Party leadership are mass activities and, therefore, should be carried out without exception, through the masses, from a mass viewpoint and on the basis of the mass line. The mass line and mass viewpoints cannot be dispensed with in any work.

Because our Party itself is a part of the people and, moreover, is dedicated to serving the people, our work in the Party is also a kind of mass work and should follow the mass line.

Because the army is also a part of the people and is likewise dedicated to serving the people, our work in the army is also a kind of mass work and should follow the mass line.

Of course, different kinds of work call for different procedure and these should not be confused with one another. For instance, forms of work in trade unions and peasant associations should be distinguished from those within the Party and the army. Nevertheless, all of these are kinds of mass work.

Naturally, the masses of the people are not all alike and our work is therefore varied and intricate. In his respective field, each comrade must directly serve a specific section of the people, such as the workers of a factory, the peasants in a village, the staff members of an office, the soldiers of an army unit, or just a few individuals. All the various kinds of work add up to the common objective of serving the Chinese people as a whole. Our comrades, therefore, must correctly grasp the relationship between the part and the whole, realizing that being directly engaged in limited activities and serving a section of the people, they are indirectly promoting and fostering the revolutionary work as a whole and serving the entire people. They must take both the part and the whole into consideration. It is wrong to keep an eye only on the part to the neglect of the whole or vice versa. The part must be integrated with the whole. When the partial, temporary interests of the people conflict with their total, long-range interests, the former must be subordinated to the latter. This means that less significant issues must be subordinated to greater issues, and minor principles to major ones. Though this is a very complicated question, our comrades will be able to follow a thoroughgoing mass line, provided they know how to use their brains to correctly distinguish and co-ordinate the limited with the basic interests of the people under all circumstances. Otherwise they may wittingly of unwittingly stand for the temporary interests of a section of the people in opposition to the long-range interests of the majority, thereby isolating themselves from the masses.

The people are generally composed of relatively active elements , intermediate elements and backward elements. In the initial stage of an undertaking the active elements are usually in the minority, while the intermediate and backward elements make up the majority. Our mass line demands consideration for the majority, that is, the intermediate and backward elements; otherwise the advanced section will become isolated and nothing can then be accomplished. The slogans for action and the forms of struggle and organization that we propose to the masses must be acceptable to the intermediate and backward elements. To foster the peoples own consciousness and initiative means chiefly fostering the consciousness and initiative of these elements. A mass movement is possible only when these people are awakened and inspired into action. We must pay particular attention to educating, uniting and organizing the active elements so that they may become the nucleus of leadership among the masses. However, it is defiantly not our intention to organize the active elements merely for their own sake, and under no circumstances must they become isolated from the intermediate and backward masses. Our aim is to draw over the intermediate and backward elements and encourage them to go into action with the help of the active elements. In other words, it is to rally the masses on a broadest possible scale. When the intermediate and backward masses are not yet awakened, we should know how to enlighten them and to patiently wait for their awakening. If, unwilling and leading just a small number of active elements, we recklessly rush forward, we shall isolate ourselves and end in failure.

Looking at the nation as a whole we see that the peasantry constitutes 80 per cent of China's population, and so consideration of the majority of the people chiefly means considering the peasantry. Our mass viewpoint is closely connected with our rural viewpoint. Under the present conditions, the Chinese working class would certainly not be able to fulfill its own tasks if it ignored Chinas peasantry or if it did not focus on the emancipation of the countryside. In view of the low cultural level of the Chinese peasants and other sections of the Chinese people (with the exception of the intelligentsia), it is all the more necessary for us to combine our general call with specific guidance in our work to set things in motion by making a breakthrough at one point. The general call alone will defiantly not succeed in guiding the masses who have a low cultural level. This is due to the fact that the masses, especially the peasantry, accept things only on the strength of their own personal experience instead of on the strength of our general propaganda and slogans. Therefore, in our work we should try to break through at a single point in order to set up a model, which the masses can see for themselves. Only through examples can we help the masses, particularly the intermediate and backward elements, to understand things, become confident and courageous and respond to the call of the Party in the form of a vigorous mass movement. Our combat heroes, our labour heroes and model workers have played an outstanding role in various places and have become the best propagandists and organizers among the masses because, through such personalities, examples and experience, the masses have come to understand things and thus enhance their consciousness and self-confidence. Similarly, revolutionary reconstruction in Chinas revolutionary base areas has played an educational and enlightening role for the whole people and has helped heighten their confidence and self-confidence. The same approach is at work whenever the leadership breaks through at one point in order to provide concrete experience for the reinforcement of the general call. It is difficult for the masses to understand a call without familiar, concrete experience to substantiate it.

Hence we must give consideration to the whole and to the majority and reject closed-doorism and sectarianism. We must maintain close ties with the masses and reject bureaucratism and warlordism.

We want to lead the masses forward but without commandism. We want to keep close ties with them, but without tailism. We should raise the consciousness of the masses and lead them forward from where there are now. In our work we must adhere to the highest principles while at the same time maintaining the closest possible ties with the masses. Such is out mass line. And while it is, of course, no easy job to carry it out, only by doing so can we become Marxists, worthy of the name Communist.

So much for the explanation of the General Programme.

5. Democratic Centralism Within the Party

Our Party is not simply an aggregate of individual members. It is a unified, organic body established according to a definite principle. It is a composite of its leaders and its rank and file. It is a unified body consisting of a headquarters (the Central Committee). Party organizations at all levels and the brad body of the membership, and it has been established in accordance with a definite principle, that is, democratic centralism in the Party.

Three individual Party members in a factory of village do not constitute a Party organization until they are organized according to the principle of democratic centralism. Under normal conditions, one of the three should be the leader of the group and the other two its members. In this way, in all activities there will be a leader and two followers. and only when this happens does such a group become the kind of Party organization which generates new strength. The strength of the proletariat lies in organization.

As laid down in the Party Constitution, democratic centralism means democracy on the basis of democracy and democracy under central guidance. It is both democratic and centralized. It embodies the relationship between the leader and the led, between higher and lower Party organizations, between individual Party members and the Party as a whole and among the Party's Central Committee. Party organizations at all levels and rank-and-file Party members.

What does it mean when we say that Party centralism is centralism based on democracy? It means that the leading bodies of the Party are elected by the membership on a democratic basis and enjoy their confidence. It means that the resolutions and policies of the Party are the crystallization of the ideas of the rank and file as expressed on a democratic basis, that they are decided on by the rank and file as expressed on a democratic basis, that they are decided upon by the rank and file or its representatives and that they are then adhered to and carried out by the leadership in conjunction with the rank and file. The authority of leading bodies of the Party is conferred by the Party membership. Therefore, these bodies are empowered to exercise centralized leadership in the management of all Party affairs on behalf of the membership and to command obedience from the organization at lower levels and from Party members. Order within the Party is built on the principle that the individual is subordinate to the organization, the minority to the majority, the lower level to the higher level and all the constituent organizations to the Central Committee. In other words, the Party''s centralism is based on, and not separated from democracy. It is not absolutism.

Why do we say the Party's democracy is democracy under centralized guidance? This means that every Party meeting is convened by a leading body and carried through under proper leadership. The adoption of every resolution or ruling is preceded by a full preparation and careful deliberation. Every election is based on a carefully prepared list of candidates. The Party as a whole has a unified Party Constitution and unified discipline for its membership to observe, and there is a unified leading body which the entire membership must observe. In other words, inner-Party democracy is not a democracy devoid of leadership., nor is it ultra-democracy, nor is it anarchy in the Party.

Democratic centralism is a discipline which unites the Party's back-bone leaders with the rank and file of the Party membership. It is a system through which to crystallize the ideas of the rank and file and to have the crystallized ideas carried out by them. It is the expression of the mass line within the Party.

Some members do not understand that centralism in the

Party is based on democracy. Consequently, they separate their leadership from inner-Party democracy and from the rank and file of the Party membership and call this "centralism". They think that their authority as leaders need not be conferred by the Party membership but can be arrogated by themselves. They think that they need not gain leading positions through election, nor need they enjoy the confidence of the Party membership and the lower Party organizations, but that they can simply proclaim themselves leaders. They think that they can arbitrarily adopt guidelines and resolutions without going through the process of pooling the ideas of the rank and file. Instead of identifying themselves with the rank and file of the Party membership, they stand above it. Instead of acting within the organization of the Party and obeying and submitting to its control, they command and control the Party and lord it over the Party organizations. With respect to their superiors, they assert independence on the pretext of preserving inner-Party democracy, while with respect to their subordinates and Party members, they suppress their democratic rights on the pretext of exercising inner-Party centralism. In fact, they neither practice democracy in dealing with their subordinates nor accept centralism in relations with their superiors. While others are obliged to adhere to resolutions adopted by the majority and observe Party discipline, they, as leaders, feel entitled to do otherwise. They observe none of such basic organizational principles as the subordination of the individual to the organization, of the minority to the majority and of the lower level to the higher level. Party rules and resolutions, in their opinion, are written for rank-and-file Party members but not for leaders. This is an anti-democratic, autocratic tendency in the Party and a reflection of the ideology characteristic of a privileged social class. It has nothing in common with our Party's centralism. It is a derivation which does, however, exist in our Party and ought to be done away with completely.

There are other comrades who, failing to understand that democracy in the Party is democracy under centralized guidance, divorce their actions from the Party's centralized leadership and from the Party as a whole. They act as they like, guided solely by their own whims and views., and they disregard the overall situation and the long range interests of the Party as a whole. They neither strictly abide by Party discipline nor carry out the decisions of the Party's leading bodies. They make all kinds of apolitical, unprincipled remarks and spread their views in disregard of organizational principles. They exaggerate things in order to sow dissention within the Party, and they indulge in endless empty talk or wrangling even during perilous emergencies. They go so far as to take advantage of the temporary confusion of some Party members who are caught unprepared, to press for votes for their own proposals in order to have their own designs carried out in the name of the "majority". These are manifestations of ultra-democracy which have nothing in common with our Party democracy. The danger of ultra-democracy, as Comrade Mao Zedong has pointed out, "lies in the fact that it damages or even completely wrecks the Party organization and weakens or even completely undermines the Party's fighting capacity."(199) It stems from "the petty-bourgeoisie's individualistic aversion to discipline. When this characteristic is brought into the Party, it develops into ultra-democratic ideas politically and organizationally. These ideas are utterly incompatible with the fighting tasks of the proletariat."(200)

Though the tendencies towards anti-democratic absolutism and ultra-democracy found in the Party are two extremes of inner-Party life, the latter often comes into being as a kind of penalty for the former. Thus wherever there is a serious tendency to absolutism, ultra-democracy is bound to rise. Both are erroneous tendencies detrimental to and destructive of genuine Party unity and solidarity. The whole Party must maintain stern vigilance against their occurrence.

We must now fully extend democracy within the Party and bring about a high degree of inner-Party democracy. At the same time, we must effect a high degree of centralism in in

Party leadership on the basis of this highly developed democracy.

In his report to the Sixth Plenary Session of the Sixth Central Committee of the Party,(167) Comrade Mao Zedong said:

> Ours is a country in which small-scale production
> and the patriarchal system prevail, and taking the
> country as a whole there is as yet no democratic life;
> consequently, this state of affairs is reflected in our
> Party by insufficient democracy in Party life. This
> phenomenon hinders the entire Party from
> exercising its initiative to the full. Similarly it has
> led to insufficient democracy in the united front and
> in the mass movements.(201)

Things are somewhat different now. Considerable progress has been made both in the democratic movement in China's liberated areas and in inner-Party democracy, especially through the rectification movement and the review of our work. The free and penetrating discussion of Party history and the Party line by cadres prior to the present Seventh National Congress represents a vigorous flourishing of inner-Party democracy and has provided adequate preparations for the Congress. However, democracy in the Party as a whole and in the local Party organizations is still inadequate and needs to be further fostered. This is why many provisions for the extension of inner-Party democracy are included in the Party Constitution.

Our Party is still waging a war and a protracted war at that. Until there are changes in our technical conditions and in the situation of our enemy, this war remains basically a kind of guerrilla war. Therefore, meetings and elections must be held where the guerrilla war permits. There should be no unwarranted curtailment of inner-Party democracy on the pretext of war.

In the Liberated Areas, Party congresses at all levels and

general membership meetings must be called, wherever possible, according to the provisions of the Constitution in order to elect the various levels of the Party's leading bodies.

The Party Constitution provides that, in the election of a leading body in the Party, in addition to the presidium of the Congress having the rights to submit a list of candidates, every delegation and every delegate is ensured the right to nominate candidates and every elector, of the right to criticize any candidates or propose alternative ones. The candidate list must be fully discussed, and the list must serve as the basis of elections conducted either by secret ballot or by open vote.

The Party Constitution provides that local Party congresses shall be convened once every two years. This means that new leading-bodies of the local Party organizations must be elected once every two years. Between congresses, however, the convocation of conferences of representatives to deliberate and decide on immediate tasks is both necessary and feasible. In the past we held cadres' meetings of various sizes to review and decide on our work; in the future we should hold congresses and conferences of representatives. Elections should be conducted no more than once every two years, because too many elections are unnecessary and handicap our work. Therefore, in addition to Party congresses, conferences of representatives are needed to review and plan or work. Such conferences may be held once or twice a year according to local Party needs, with representatives selected by the lower Party committees. Such a conference has the power to remove or replace members of Party committees or to add further members through bi-elections. but its resolutions and the removal, replacement or addition of Party committee members must be approved by the Party committee in question. The reason for this is that the conference is subordinate to the Party committee, although its power is greater than that of the cadres' meetings of the past.

Party congresses and conferences at the provincial or boarder regional,(63) regional, county or district levels may be held in rotation For instance this year, congresses at the provincial or border regional and county levels may be held at the same time as conferences at the regional and district levels are held. This should then be reversed the next year.

The Party committees at various levels should be broadened to include people in charge of various fields of work as well as cadres who maintain close ties with the masses. According to the Constitution, a standing committee should be formed in each Party committee to take charge of the day-to-day work. Similarly, the standing committee should include leading cadres in various fields of work so that it may function as a regular leading nucleus of each of the different kinds of work in the locality. A Party committee may, when necessary, avail itself of one or two assistant secretaries to help the secretary and to ensure that nothing is neglected. The committee is not designed to just do inner-Party organizational work but should serve as the body which directs all the activities in its locality. (Inner-Party organizational work is only part of its activities and should and should be specially assigned to its organizational department.) Therefore, decisions and plans of a general character should be made only after being discussed at committee meetings. And after discussions are reached, individuals should be assigned to put them into effect.

The effort to encourage criticism and self-criticism among Party members and cadres is a crucial factor in extending inner-Party democracy. Comrade Mao Zedong stresses the importance of self-criticism in his report by pointing out that the conscientious practice of self-criticism is a hallmark distinguishing our Party from other political parties. We must develop a positive sense of responsibility among our Party members and cadres with regard to our Party's policies and work, and we must encourage them to use their brains to raise questions boldly and express their views to the point. To this end, those in charge of the leading bodies at all levels must be the first to make detailed self-criticism of the shortcomings and mistakes found in the work under their leadership. They must set an example to the Party membership and the cadres by being fully prepared in their minds to accept criticism from others, without being upset or impatient and without resorting to repressing of punishing their critics. This is the only way to foster inner-Party democracy with success. Without such an approach, Party congresses and conferences, even if regularly convened, must be lifeless, undemocratic gatherings filled with dull and repetitious speeches and purely routine voting. Many of our comrades, including some in responsible positions, still do not know how to conduct a successful meeting. As a result, many meetings have ended in failure or produced poor results, and sometimes meetings become a heavy burden on Party membership and the masses. Clearly, holding meetings does not in itself constitute democracy. They must be well conducted so that they are permeated with democracy, criticism and self-criticism. For guidance in this area we must observe Comrade Mao Zedong's directive in the "Resolution of the Gutian Meeting", which deals with the question of how to kindle the Party members' interest in attending meetings.

Experience proves that whenever a leading comrade undertakes sincere and necessary self-criticism in public, the Party members and the people will develop their own criticism and self-criticism, have greater initiative and better unity, overcome their shortcomings and improve their work. At the same time the comrade's prestige is augmented instead of being impaired. This has been borne out by a great deal of experience both in the Party and among the masses. On the other hand,, whenever a leading comrade, lacking the spirit of self-criticism, refuses or fears to criticize or reveal his own short-comings or mistakes and tries to cover them up or, failing to be pleased, to learn of his mistakes or to express gratitude for the criticism, becomes flushed with anger, makes acrimonious retorts and looks for chances to take revenge on his critics, in that place the Party members and the people are unable to foster democracy or self-criticism, they lack initiative and unity and they are unable to overcome their short-comings and improve their work. This, of course, causes the leading comrades to lose prestige. Therefore the leading personnel of all local Party organizations have a tremendous responsibility for the promotion and broadening of democracy within the Party.

The Party Constitution provides that the leading bodies and the personnel of the Party organizations at all levels should regularly report on their work to the Party members and lower Party organizations that have elected them. In every such report they should not only discuss the current situation and the successes but also the shortcomings, weaknesses and mistakes, and they should request comments and criticisms from the electors and the lower Party organizations. Experience shows that the responsibility for errors and shortcomings in the work of many lower Party organizations or cadres rest not with them but with the higher leading bodies. Many such errors and shortcomings are due to the failure of the higher leading bodies to assign tasks and clarify policies at the right moment. Even when they have done this, errors are still caused by their failure to be systematic and thorough with the pertinent problems, or by the fact that the very tasks and policies that they worked out are erroneous. In such cases, it is not permissible to shift the responsibility onto, or lay blame on, the lower Party organizations or Party members and cadres, because such action destroys their confidence and crushes their initiative. Of course, lower Party committees, Party members and cadres must, on their part, show a similar spirit of self-criticism towards their own shortcomings and mistakes.

The essential aim of inner-Party democracy is to promote the initiative and activity of the Party members, raise their sense of responsibility towards the cause of the Party and encourage them on their representatives to voice their views fully, within the frame work of the Party Constitution. In this way they can take an active part in the Party's leadership of the people's cause and help strengthen the unity and discipline of the Party. Only through a genuine extension of inner-Party democracy can voluntary Party discipline be strengthened, inner-Party centralism established and consolidated and correct leadership given by the leading bodies. Therefore, the Party Constitution provides that the leading bodies of the Party at all levels shall carry on their work in accordance with the principle of inner-Party democracy.

Giving reign to a high degree of democracy within the Party does not mean weakening inner-Party centralism in any way. On the contrary, we intend to bring about a high degree of centralism on the basis of a high degree of democracy. The two should be combined and not be counterposed. Centralized leadership cannot be attained without the latter which can prevail only under a democratically based and highly centralized leadership. It is wrong to hold that centralized leadership will be weakened by a high degree of democracy. Thus, the Constitution provides that, in performing their functions in accordance with the principle of inner-Party democracy, the leading bodies at all levels should not hamper inner-Party centralism or misconstrue as anarchistic tendencies (such as ascertations of "independence" or ultra-democracy) any inner-Party democracy legitimate and beneficial to centralized action.

We must see to it that inner-Party democracy contributes to the cause of the Party, which is the cause of the people, and that it neither weakens the fighting will and unity of the Party nor becomes a tool for saboteurs, anti-Party elements, splitters, time-servers and careerists. Thus the Constitution provides that a thorough review of, and debate on, the policy and line of the whole Party or of a local Party organization may be conducted only under proper guidance and when time permits, that is to say, not in times of emergency. It must be based on the resolutions of the Central Committee of the Party or of the local leading bodies as the case may be. Such a review can be conducted based on a proposal by more than one half of the members of the lower Party organizations or a proposal by a higher organization.

Inner-Party democracy must be broadened, but Party resolutions must be put into effect unconditionally. The subordination of the individual to the organization, of the lower level to the higher level, of the minority to the majority and of all the constituent Party organizations to the Central Committee — this principle laid down in the Constitution must be observed unconditionally.

Some comrades might impose such conditions as refusing to adhere the resolutions or instructions unless they consider them correct, unless they think that their superior is qualified in terms ability, rank, length of Party membership or cultural level, or unless the leader has treated them well or belongs to the same -group". It must be pointed out that such conditions are unjustifiable. A Communist expresses how keen his sense of discipline is and how strictly he observes discipline precisely when he is in danger or when serious differences arise between him and the Party organization over issues of principle or relations among comrades. It is only when he unconditionally carries out organizational principles from a minority position that he can be considered a Party member with a keen sense of discipline and principle, who looks at the total situation and knows that local interests should be subordinate to overall interests, less significant issues to greater issues, and that specific differences of principle and differences over relations among comrades should be subordinate the supreme interests of Party unity and Party discipline.

Under no circumstances should we Communists encourage blind obedience. Since we are now in the midst of guerrilla warfare conducted over vast rural areas and since the conditions differ widely inside and outside these areas, we should peruse a policy of "decentralised operations under centralized leadership" in our work. Policies which either over-centralize operations or put decentralized operations and centralized leadership on an equal footing are erroneous. By decentralized operations, we do not mean assertations of "independence"; we mean independent actions and the ability to operate independently. Rather than being separated from centralized leadership, decentralized operations must be put under it. Conditions being what they are, it often happens that the decisions and instructions of a leading body are necessarily of a general character and so fail to cover the conditions in all places. Consequently, while applicable to ordinary areas, such decisions and instructions suit certain special areas, and it also often happens that they contain mistakes and are impracticable. In such cases, we should not advocate blind implementation or obedience. Instead, we should encourage intelligent and conscientious action which calls for serious study of the circumstances, the decisions and instructions. When we find that they contain mistakes or are at variance with the local situation, we should have the courage to bring the matter to the attention of a higher body with a request for their withdrawal or a amendment. We should not enforce them blindly and obstinately, for this will lead to a waste of money and manpower and isolate us from the masses. By pointing to mistakes, a subordinate is by no means being disobedient to his superior, nor is he asserting "independence", but is conscientiously carrying out decisions and instructions. Such Party members are the best Party members, for they are capable not merely of independent deliberation but of also helping to correct the errors and shortcomings of the higher body. They should be especially commended. There are three possible approaches towards the decisions and instructions of the higher bodies. The first is to carry out those decisions and instructions which appeal to you and ignore those which do not. This is an assertion of "independence" pure and simple, whatever the pretext and must not be permitted. The second is to carry them out blindly and mechanically, without taking the trouble to study them or the specific circumstances. This is a blind rather than a careful implementation of the decisions and instructions of a higher body and is consequently also impermissible. And the third is to study both the circumstances and the decisions and instructions, to resolutely carry out what is practicable and to report what is impracticable to the higher body, giving detailed reasons and requesting amendments. This is the way to carry out decisions and instructions intelligently and conscientiously, and it is the only correct approach. Not only do we not oppose, but we should by every means encourage, this initiative and activity on the part of every Party member. While opposing any disregard for discipline or assertion of "independence", the Party encourages the initiative of every member in tackling problems and doing work independently under the guidance of the Party line.

A leading body should allow its lower organizations and members to make suggestions, raise questions and propose revisions with regard to its decisions and instructions which, when the existence of shortcomings or mistakes is substantiated, should be corrected accordingly. If the lower ranks are wrong, a satisfactory explanation should be given to straighten out their ideas, and no harsh measures should be taken against them. If the higher body insists the execution of a decision or instruction despite the appeals for revision, then it should be carried out and the lower ranks must not persist in their own stand of resist the decision.

The discipline of the Communist Party is based on voluntary subordination. It should not be turned into something mechanical, which restricts the activity and initiative of the membership. The sense of discipline and the initiative of the membership should go hand in hand.

The Party Constitution provides that a Party organization at every level shall ensure that the publications under the guidance disseminate the decisions and policies of higher organizations and of the central organs. This is necessitated by the Party's unified and national character. Decisions and policies should be disseminated in all places, while conflicting ideas should not be publicized at all Marxist ideology should be disseminated while ideologies contrary to it should not. This task is not being satisfactorily performed by some of our lower Party organizations. Some papers have failed to give sufficient publicity to the decisions and policies of the Central Committee

71

and have sometimes even carried articles at variance with them. Party organizations at all levels must check up on this and make corrections.

With regard to national issues, the Party Constitution provides that prior to a statement or decision by the Central Committee, no lower Party organizations or their leading personnel shall take the liberty of making public their views or decisions on such issues, although they may hold discussions among themselves and put forward their proposals to the Central Committee. This is necessary to ensure the Party's unified and national character. The Party as a whole can have but one orientation or line to follow, not several. Lower Party organizations should not exceed their powers by making their views public in place of, or prior to the Central Committee on those issues which the Committee should and must decide upon and make public. No leading comrade in the Party, including members of the Central Committee, should publicise their views on issues of a national character without the Central Committee's approval. While they may discuss their views at the meetings of local Party committees and make suggestions to the Central Committee, it is impermissible for them to make public, either inside or outside the Party, views not yet made known by the Central Committee, or to dispatch circular messages among other local Party committees for the dissemination of these views. The reason for this is that, should such views or decisions conflict with those of the Central Committee, this would adversely affect the Party and the people and aid our enemies. When we lacked or were short of radio facilities, we didn't stress this point. But now that such facilities are in general use, it must be emphasised. The Central Committee has called attention to this a number of times during the War of Resistance Against Japan.

Concerning local questions, the Constitution authorizes lower Party organizations to make independent decisions, provided these decisions do not conflict with those of the Central Committee or of other higher organizations. In this connection, higher organizations should, on their part, avoid interfering in the affairs of lower organizations and refrain from making decisions for them. While it is necessary for a higher body to make suggestions to a lower organization in order to help it to resolve questions correctly, the power of decision must rest with the latter.

Our Party organizations are still working underground in many areas. In such circumstances they must adopt special forms to carry out their tasks. Hence the Constitution provides that those organizational forms and methods of work which are suited to overt Party organizations but not to the covert ones may be modified. This provision is necessary. Organizational principles provided in the Constitution must be carried out by the whole Party, but the organizational forms and methods of work should be changed according to changing circumstances and conditions. This point has been already dealt with.

www.ingramcontent.com/pod-product-compliance
Lightning Source LLC
Chambersburg PA
CBHW060211290526
45789CB00003B/1238